4/2010

NORTH CAROLINA

NAN ALEX

Consultants

MELISSA N. MATUSEVICH, PH.D.

Curriculum and Instruction Specialist
Blacksburg, Virginia

MEL BURTON

Children's Information Specialist
Public Library of Charlotte and Mecklenburg County
Charlotte, North Carolina

CHILDREN'S PRESS®

AN IMPRINT OF SCHOLASTIC INC.

New York · Toronto · London · Auckland · Sydney · Mexico City
New Delhi · Hong Kong · Danbury, Connecticut

North Carolina is in the southeastern part of the United States. It is bordered by Tennessee, Virginia, South Carolina, Georgia, and the Atlantic Ocean.

Project Editor: Meredith DeSousa
Art Director: Marie O'Neill
Photo Researcher: Marybeth Kavanagh
Design: Robin West, Ox and Company, Inc.
Page 6 map and recipe art: Susan Hunt Yule
All other maps: XNR Productions, Inc.

Library of Congress Cataloging-in-Publication Data
Alex, Nan.
      North Carolina / by Nan Alex.
         p. cm.—(From sea to shining sea)
      Includes bibliographical references and index.
      ISBN-10 0-531-18808-6
      ISBN-13 978-0-531-18808-8
1. North Carolina—Juvenile literature. [1. North Carolina.] I. Title. II. Series

F254.3 .A44 2008
975.6—dc22   2007042639

TABLE of CONTENTS

CHAPTER ONE

INTRODUCING THE TAR HEEL STATE

Tourists flock to the beaches near Cape Hatteras Lighthouse, where you can find some of the best fishing and surfing on the east coast.

North Carolina is a unique state for many reasons. Although it's not a big state, more people live in North Carolina than in many other states. Also, forests grow near the coast because sand dunes block the spray of the ocean's harmful saltwater. Third, the state has some unusual wildlife, including rare fish and birds. Fourth, the state's climate is so changeable. Part of North Carolina may be subtropical, or very hot and humid, while another part may be as cold as southern Canada.

The state has two nicknames—the Tar Heel State and Old North State. The first nickname says a lot about the people of North Carolina. Southern Soldiers who refused to retreat during the Civil War were known as "tar heels." The nickname referred to the tar supposedly stuck to the soldiers' shoes. It became a badge of bravery. The tar was made from the state's once great forests of long-leaf pine. The second nickname sets North Carolina apart from the other Carolina to the south.

Since colonial days, North Carolina has played an important part in

9 Nov 99

Blackbird

Heron

Grebe

Dragonfly

Bullfrog

Diving
Beetle

Muskrat

Year by year, the pond itself also changes. Water plants in and around the marsh shed leaves. The leaves slowly decay, making new soil on land, new mud in the water. The edges of the marsh become drier. Maybe trees and bushes grow. The pond gets shallower. In time, plants grow farther out in the pond or all the way across.

Years pass. What was once a pond and marsh becomes a tree-bordered meadow—unless floods come to scour the pond, unless muskrats munch cattails faster than they can grow back, unless beavers dam the river, making a new pond. Nature is not fixed. Change is natural.

Will your pond be different next year? There is only one way to find out!

Links of Life

A breeze ruffles the bright yellow cottonwoods. Leaves swirl. Puffs of cattail seeds drift through the air like snow. There is a chill in the wind and a hint of winter. The pond is quieter now than it was in spring. No frogs call. No insects chirp. Few birds trill their sweet songs. What is happening?

Many summer birds have flown south. Insects to eat are in short supply. Frogs, toads, and turtles have settled into the mud underwater or underground. Fish, dragonfly larvae, and tadpoles hang out in the waterweed jungle, scarcely moving. As seasons change, animals' lives change in and around the pond.

Tracks

Did you notice tracks or prints on some pages? They are life-size. Measure them with your hand to test the size of the animals' feet.

Treasure Maps

Front map: Find the mud flats where Heron fished. Find Blackbird's cattail patch.

Back map: Which animals use the island? Which animal uses the smallest space?

Breath of Life

We use our lungs to breathe oxygen from the air. Pond animals get oxygen in many ways. Do you remember which animal . . .

- Used both lungs *and* slimy skin to breathe?
- Breathed through its tail and jetted away?
- Breathed through a snorkel-tail?
- Carried a bubble of air under its wings?

Mini-Monsters

You may think the "monsters" in the waterweed jungle are wild! If you magnify a drop of pond water, the mini-monsters you see are even wilder— and important first links of the food chain.

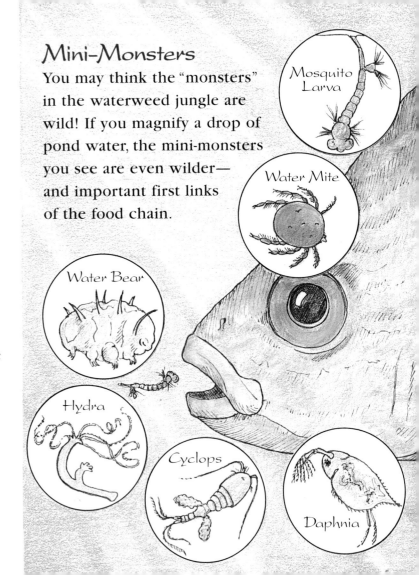

Mosquito Larva

Water Mite

Water Bear

Hydra

Cyclops

Daphnia

American history. North Carolina was the first colony to vote for independence from Great Britain. North Carolina's fight for the rights of its citizens ended in victory for all Americans.

What else comes to mind when you think of North Carolina?

* Cape Hatteras National Seashore, the longest beach on the east coast
* Dinosaur bones on display at the North Carolina Museum of Natural Sciences
* Salamanders at Great Smoky Mountains National Park, the "Salamander Capital of the World"
* The mysterious Lost Colony at Roanoke
* African Americans protesting at a lunch counter in Greensboro
* A plate of just-fried hush puppies
* Handmade furniture at High Point, the "Home Furnishings Capital of the World"
* The first succesful heavier-than-air flight at Kitty Hawk
* Reed Gold Mine, where twelve-year-old Conrad Reed's discovery of gold started the first gold rush

The Tar Heel State is special in many ways. In this book, you'll find out why. This is the story of North Carolina.

Virginia

Tennessee

Georgia

South Carolina

ALBEMARLE SOUND

PAMLICO RIVER

PAMLICO SOUND

ATLANTIC OCEAN

LITTLE TENNESSEE RIVER

©SHY01

•Asheville

Winston-Salem•

High Point•

LAKE NORMAN

•Charlotte

PEE DEE RIVER

Greensboro•

Durham•

★ Raleigh

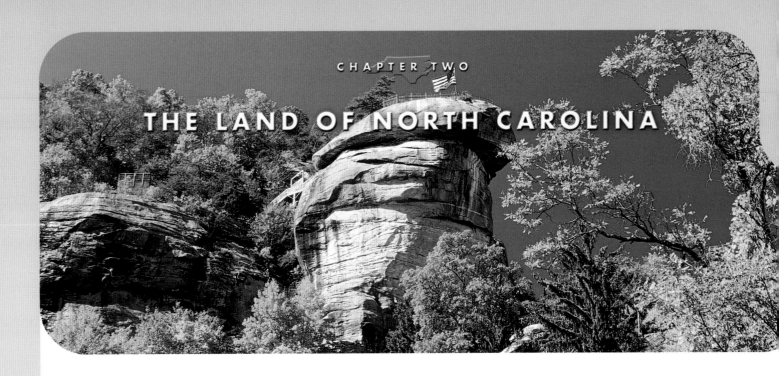

CHAPTER TWO

THE LAND OF NORTH CAROLINA

Just where is North Carolina? It is located along the southern half of the Atlantic seaboard in the eastern United States. To the west of North Carolina lies Tennessee. To the north is Virginia, and to the south are South Carolina and Georgia. These states, together with Alabama, form the region known as the Southeast.

From east to west, the land of North Carolina rises gradually. The state is divided into four land regions: the Atlantic Coastal Plain, the Outer Banks, the Piedmont, and the Mountains.

Autumn is a great time to visit Chimney Rock Park, where you can catch the view, hike the trails, and stop in at the nature center.

THE ATLANTIC COASTAL PLAIN

The Atlantic Coastal Plain is the largest natural region in the state. It covers 25,000 square miles (64,750 square kilometers). As you travel inland about 100 miles (161 km), the area is flat and mostly swampy.

One of the swamplands, the Dismal Swamp, has eerie-looking black gum trees and cypress trees covered with moss. This swamp covers 600 square miles (1,554 sq km) of the northeastern part of the state and spreads into Virginia. Lake Drummond is one of many lakes in this area. Unusual lights, called foxfire, have been seen around this lake at night. The lights come from decaying forest wood that gives off gas. Beyond the swamp, the land becomes flat for the next hundred miles (161 km) to the west.

Dismal Swamp is a haven for birds and mammals. Many rare plants can be found there as well.

THE OUTER BANKS

The Outer Banks are a string of islands that run along the coast of North Carolina. They are called barrier islands because they protect the mainland from hurri-

EXTRA! EXTRA!

The Cape Hatteras Lighthouse is the tallest in the nation and is a famous symbol of North Carolina. Built in 1871, this 20-story-high lighthouse stands 208 feet (63 m) tall. Its light can be seen for over 20 miles (32 km), and it has helped sailors to navigate the sea for over 100 years. In 1999 the Atlantic Ocean threatened the lighthouse, as the tide came in closer and closer. The entire lighthouse was moved back 2900 feet (884 m) in June 1999. Today it is open to the public and you can climb all the way to the top.

The Outer Banks stick out from the coast in the shape of a foot.

FIND OUT MORE

The environment of the Outer Banks is sandy and salty. Plants do not usually grow well in such an environment. Yet more than 300 kinds of plants exist in Nags Head Woods, a maritime forest on the Outer Banks. What makes this possible?

canes. Like one long foot, the coastline stretches 300 miles (483 km) from Virginia to South Carolina.

The "heel" of the foot kicks out into the ocean at three points—Cape Hatteras, Cape Lookout, and Cape Fear. Many hurricanes and other fierce storms have struck Cape Hatteras. Hundreds of ships have sunk in the surrounding waters. This explains how Cape Hatteras got its nickname—the "Graveyard of the Atlantic."

THE PIEDMONT

The central part of the state is called the Piedmont, or the foothills of North Carolina. The Piedmont rises gently upward from the coastal

9

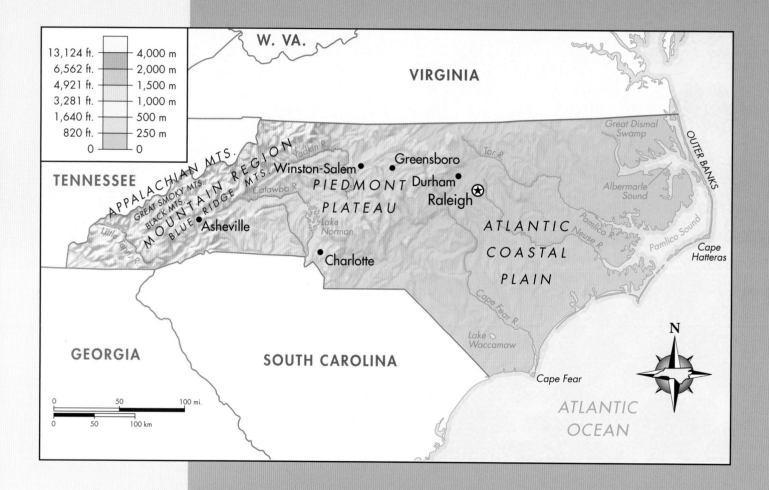

W. VA.

VIRGINIA

TENNESSEE

13,124 ft.	4,000 m
6,562 ft.	2,000 m
4,921 ft.	1,500 m
3,281 ft.	1,000 m
1,640 ft.	500 m
820 ft.	250 m
0	0

Great Dismal
Swamp

OUTER BANKS

APPALACHIAN MTS.
GREAT SMOKY MTS.
BLACK MTS.
MOUNTAIN REGION
BLUE RIDGE MTS.

Yadkin R.

Tar R.

Albermarle
Sound

Winston-Salem
Greensboro
Durham
Raleigh

PIEDMONT
PLATEAU

Catawba R.

Little Tenn. R.

Asheville

Lake
Norman

ATLANTIC
COASTAL
PLAIN

Pamlico R.

Neuse R.

Pamlico Sound

Cape
Hatteras

Charlotte

GEORGIA

SOUTH CAROLINA

Cape Fear R.

Lake
Waccamaw

Cape Fear

N

ATLANTIC
OCEAN

0   50   100 mi.
0   50   100 km

plain. An imaginary border known as the fall line divides the two regions. The land is higher to the west of the fall line, causing many waterfalls.

More people live in the Piedmont than anywhere else in the state. That's because most of North Carolina's major cities are located here, including Raleigh and Charlotte. Much of the state's manufacturing takes place in the Piedmont.

Many people live in scenic, rural communities in the Piedmont region of North Carolina.

THE MOUNTAINS

The mountains of western North Carolina begin where the Piedmont ends. These mountains are the southern part of the Appalachian Mountains that run from Pennsylvania to Georgia. North Carolina has two important mountain chains—the Blue Ridge Mountains and the Great Smoky Mountains. These are connected by other mountain ranges, including the Black Mountains. The dark evergreen forests across the peaks give the Black Mountains their name. They are the highest mountains east of the Mississippi River.

The Appalachian Trail follows the crest of Roan Mountain in North Carolina. Many people think that Roan Mountain is the most beautiful part of the Trail. The Trail is part of a path that is almost as long as the

FIND OUT MORE

Mount Mitchell was named after Dr. Elisha Mitchell, a professor of science at the University of North Carolina. In 1835 he discovered that this mountain was higher than Grandfather Mountain, which was thought to be the highest mountain in the region. Grandfather Mountain is 5,964 feet (1,818 m) high at its highest point, Calloway Peak. Mount Mitchell is 6,684 feet (2,037 m) high, the highest point in eastern America. How much higher is Mount Mitchell than Grandfather Mountain?

The Blue Ridge Parkway is 469 miles (755 km) of road that winds its way through the Appalachian region in North Carolina and Virginia.

Roan Mountain is one of the most beautiful mountains in the southern Appalachians. Roan Mountain State Park has eight hiking trails covering 17 miles (27 km).

United States is wide. It stretches 2,100 miles (3,380 km) from Georgia to Maine. Roan Mountain gets its name from the rhododendrons that bloom there in late spring.

LAKES AND RIVERS

North Carolina has many lakes. Some of these lakes have been formed by dams that hold back river water. Companies like the Tennessee Valley Authority create lakes for the purpose of providing water power for electricity. The lakes also help control flooding.

In the coastal plain east of the fall line, there are natural lakes. Mattamuskeet is the state's largest natural lake. It is 15 miles (24 km) long and 6 miles (10 km) wide. Other lakes are in shallow, sunken areas known as the Carolina Bays. Some people believe that a meteor fell thousands of years ago from outer space and landed on the earth so hard that it broke into pieces and created these holes. Over time, these holes filled with water and formed lakes.

Many rivers start in the mountains. In the coastal plain, the rivers slow down. The Roanoke, Neuse, Tar-Pamlico, and Cape Fear Rivers are the major rivers of the state. The Roanoke River is the

The oval shape of a Carolina Bay can be seen perfectly from the air. Carolina Bays are believed to be at least 30,000 to 100,000 years old!

Whitewater Falls in Nantahala National Forest is one of the highest falls east of the Mississippi.

opposite:
The bald cypress thrives in swamp water.

longest. It flows into Albemarle Sound in the northeastern part of the state. The Neuse and Tar Rivers in central North Carolina and Cape Fear River and South River all flow into the Atlantic Ocean. Cape Fear River is the only one that empties directly into the ocean. The Hiwasee, Little Tennessee, and Watauga Rivers flow westward from the mountains.

The Blue Ridge Mountain chain receives more than 40 inches (102 cm) of rain a year. Rainwater fills the creeks, which run into rivers, picking up speed as they flow down slopes. They roar over waterfalls, turning into whitewater rapids. Whitewater Falls is one of the largest waterfalls in the United States. It's about as tall as the Empire State Building in New York City.

Most of the lakes in western North Carolina were built by human hands. The largest is Lake Norman on the Catawba River in the west central part of the state. Other lakes include High Rock Lake on the Yadkin River, Roanoke Rapids Lake on the Roanoke River, and Roxboro Lake on the northern border of Virginia.

Between the Atlantic Ocean and the eastern border of North Carolina's mainland lie Currituck Sound, Albemarle Sound, and Pamlico Sound. Farther south are Raleigh Bay and Onslow Bay. Cape Fear is located near the southernmost end of the state.

If you travel from the Outer Banks to the mountains, you'll find a whole range of plant life. The dunes of the Outer Banks are full of low shrubs such as sea oats. Trees can't survive the high ocean winds.

The wetlands lie to the west of the Outer Banks. Here you'll find salt marshes and freshwater marshes with grasses and cattails. Bald cypress trees that are 2,000 years old are in the swamps.

In the Sandhills located to the southwest of Raleigh, the soil is too sandy for plants to grow. In fact, the Sandhills were once beaches. The grass is wiry, and any flowers that grow here don't need much rain.

You'll find many forests throughout the state. The great Nantahala National Forest in the southwest has many waterfalls and whitewater rapids. Buxton Woods is the largest maritime forest in the Outer Banks.

There is less wildlife in North Carolina than there used to be because of logging and building. Still, the state has about 850 species of vertebrates, or animals and birds with a backbone, living there. Some of these animals and birds live in the Outer Banks year-round. Ducks, geese, and tundra swans come during the winter months. Herons and egrets spend the summer months here. You might also see peregrine falcons and bald eagles. Alligators live in the

Spotted salamanders are, in fact, hard to spot! They spend most of the year beneath forest litter or under the ground, and rarely come out during the day.

swamps while beavers and muskrats build their homes in the rivers. On land are rabbits, deer, squirrels, and chipmunks. Black bears and red wolves are also found in wildlife refuges like the Great Dismal Swamp.

If you head west into the Appalachian Mountains you'll be in the "Salamander Capital of the World." Salamanders thrive in moist soil, which makes the southeastern United States an ideal home. The Great Smoky Mountains National Park is crawling with salamanders. But you won't see them very often because they like to hide in rotting tree stumps, burrowed in the ground or under rocks, leaves, or logs.

Lake Waccamaw has many species of fish and mollusks. The Waccamaw silverside is only found in this lake. Jordan Lake in central North Carolina just west of Raleigh is also well known, but not for its fish—rare bald eagles nest in the upper regions.

CLIMATE

North Carolina weather can go to extremes. On some summer days, temperatures can top 100°Fahrenheit (37.8°Celsius) while winter temperatures may drop below zero (−18°C). Temperatures are naturally higher on the coast. The Gulf Stream warms areas south of Wilmington. But if you travel through the Piedmont to the mountains you'll feel the cool air. Some of the state's highest points can be as cold as southern Canada, more than 3,000 miles (4,827 km) away.

FIND OUT MORE

In the 1920s, European wild boars were brought to a private game preserve near the Great Smoky Mountains National Park. It wasn't long before the animals escaped and wandered into the park. How do you think they affected the balance of life in the park?

Overall, North Carolina has a mild climate, thanks to the Gulf Stream and the Blue Ridge Mountains. The Gulf Stream keeps the coastal areas mild while the mountains shield the region to the east from the cold weather of the north and northwest. The annual mean temperature in January is 40°F (4°C). In July, the annual mean temperature is 76°F (24°C).

North Carolina receives 40 to 80 inches (102 to 203 cm) of precipitation each year. The town of Cashiers gets the most rain—about 80 inches (203 cm) a year. It's the wettest place in the eastern United States! Scientists say that a tropical storm or hurricane strikes North Carolina once every four years. In September 1999, Hurricane Floyd hit the North Carolina coast with high winds and flooding.

Fierce hurricanes sometimes strike the Outer Banks, destroying many homes.

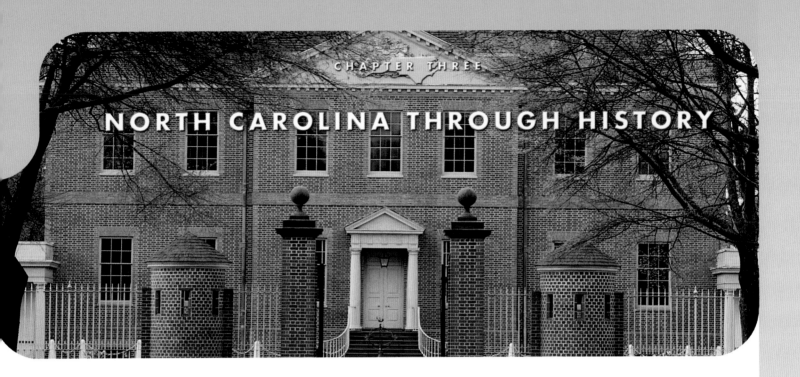

CHAPTER THREE

NORTH CAROLINA THROUGH HISTORY

Tryon Palace, built in 1767, was named after William Tryon, a royal governor in 1765. Today you can take a tour of the palace and its gardens.

The story of North Carolina began thousands of years ago. At that time, Paleo Indians made their way across a land bridge from Asia to North America. They traveled southward and eastward hunting for buffalo and small game.

Scientists say that the first hunters reached North Carolina 11,000 years ago as the last Ice Age came to an end. The hunters settled in villages near rivers or streams. There was fresh water to drink and plenty of fish to eat. The hunters built shelters called wigwams by bending young trees and covering the trees with bark and hides. They cleared fields and planted squash, corn, and other vegetables.

Over time, Native American tribes developed and spread throughout the territory. Among these tribes were the Tuscarora, the Catawba, and the Cherokee. The Tuscaroras built their villages along the Roanoke, Pamlico, and Neuse Rivers. The English described the tribe as hostile and warlike. The Tuscaroras lived on the coastal plain until 1713, when they moved to join relatives in New York state.

The Catawba tribe settled in the Piedmont. They did not move from place to place but settled down to farm the land. Their houses were made of bark with roofs of cattails. They lived peacefully with the new settlers.

The Cherokees, the largest tribe, lived in the mountains. At first, the Cherokees lived in huts, then log hogans, wooden houses covered with hardened clay. Like the Catawba, the Cherokee tribe did not wander but settled in communities. The taller, stronger Cherokees traveled a long way to hunt for wild game, but they always came home.

The earliest Cherokee lived in what is now the western part of the state. Today, a small number of Cherokee still live in the mountains of North Carolina.

THE EUROPEANS ARRIVE

It is likely that a man named Giovanni da Verrazzano was the first European explorer to set sight on what is now North Carolina. King Francis I of France sent out an expedition to explore across the Atlantic, and he chose Verrazzano as its leader. Verrazzano set sail with four ships and reached the coast with just one ship left in 1524. He ran into trouble on the sand banks and could not find a place to anchor his ship. So he sailed on to explore the area between Cape Fear and Kitty Hawk. Spain

This painting shows Raleigh onboard his ship during one of his voyages of discovery.

sent explorers to North Carolina a few years after France, but neither the French nor the Spanish tried to colonize the area.

In 1584, Queen Elizabeth of England appointed Sir Walter Raleigh to arrange an expedition. The explorers reached Cape Hatteras that summer and claimed the land for England. They stayed on Roanoke Island and traveled up and down the coast. They wrote reports. They drew pictures. They brought two natives, Manteo and Wanchese, back to England. Coming from the strange New World, the natives drew much attention. News of the discoveries—the crops, the fish, and the wildlife—spread throughout England. Plans to colonize the area of North Carolina grew quickly. Rich men hoping for trade offered money and supplies to Raleigh. Between 1584 and 1585, the territory was named Virginia for Queen Elizabeth, the Virgin Queen.

The same year, another fleet of ships set sail for North Carolina under Sir Richard Grenville. Most of the 107 colonists were soldiers. A few of them were merchants and "gentlemen." An artist, John White, was with them along with Raleigh's friend, a scientist, Thomas Hariot. They made maps of the area. White drew pictures of the natives as well as the plants and other living things. Even today, White's watercolor drawings are one of the most valuable sources of information about these early voyages.

The colonists built a fort and some small houses at the northern end of Roanoke Island. When supplies ran out, Grenville, along with White and Hariot, returned to England for more. When White made his next journey back to Roanoke Island he was appointed governor. He sailed with a group of 113 settlers, including seventeen women and eleven children. When they finally arrived on the island years later, the original colony had mysteriously disappeared—only skeletons were found. The only clue was the word CROATOAN carved on a tree. To this day, no one knows what happened to the colonists.

Two children were born on Roanoke in 1587, including White's granddaughter, Virginia Dare. Virginia was the first child born of English parents in the new world. She, too, disappeared along with the rest of the colonists on Roanoke.

The only clue left on Roanoke Island was the word CROATOAN carved into a tree.

THE FIRST SETTLERS

In 1629, King Charles I of England gave Sir Robert Heath a charter to the entire southern part of Britain's claim to America. Heath was the king's legal adviser and named the new territory *New Carolana* after King Charles. This area included both North Carolina and South Carolina.

In 1663, King Charles II took the Carolina charter away from Heath and gave it to eight of his friends, who were called Lords Proprietors. These ruling landowners did not want to leave their homes in England, so they ruled the colony from England by appointing governors to act on their behalf.

The colonists, however, did not want to be governed by England. In Albemarle, the colonists arrested their governor in 1677 and elected John Culpeper, a land surveyor, to govern the colony. For two years Culpeper acted as governor until he was finally removed by the English landowners.

By 1680, 5,000 new settlers had arrived. They were poor farmers who moved into areas occupied by Native American tribes. In 1706 the first permanent town of Bath was established. Five years later, the Tuscarora tribe rose up against the settlers and killed many of them. The Tuscarora War of 1711 raged on for eighteen months. The Tuscaroras burned the settlers' homes, destroyed their crops, and drove off or

WHAT'S IN A NAME?

Many names of places in North Carolina have interesting origins.

Name	Comes from or means
Carolina	Carolus is Latin for "Charles"
Kitty Hawk	Poteskeet word meaning "Chickahauk"
Charlotte	Queen Charlotte, wife of Britain's King George III
Cape Hatteras	Hatteras Native Americans
Raleigh	Sir Walter Raleigh, English explorer
Mount Mitchell	Dr. Elisha Mitchell, science professor
Roanoke River	Roanoke Native Americans
Catawba River	Catawba Native Americans
Tar River	tar, forest product

killed livestock. In the end, many Tuscaroras were captured, killed, or sold into slavery as a result of the war.

Throughout the early 1700s, pirates also raided the coastal towns. One of the most famous pirates was Edward Teach, known as Blackbeard. He was killed in a battle near Ocracoke Island in 1718. Some believe that Blackbeard's stolen treasure is still buried there.

To keep the growing colony successful, indentured servants were hired for a period of four to seven years to work the farms. Some servants were paid for their work. As the colony grew, more and more servants were needed. Plantation owners, people who owned large pieces of land, began importing people from Africa to work as slaves. Slaves were not paid for their work, and they were "owned" by their master, the landowner. Enslaved Africans worked on plantations for their entire lives.

In 1729 the Lords Proprietors sold their interests in the colony to King George II. It then became a royal colony ruled by the king's governor. Settlers from Britain and other colonies filled the territory. Many came from Pennsylvania, Virginia, and South Carolina. North Carolina's population grew rapidly. By 1750, North Carolina had 75,000 people. By 1775, the number of people living there reached 350,000.

THE PATH TO FREEDOM

Throughout the colonization of America, there were many wars. The British and the French fought over the same land. The French and the Spanish fought over the southern part of North Carolina. The settlers

Blackbeard was the most feared pirate on the high seas. He was eventually killed in battle with the Royal Navy.

Parts of the French and Indian War were fought in North Carolina. Fort Dobbs was the scene of an important victory for the British.

fought with Native Americans. Some Native Americans sided with the British; others, with the French. In 1754 war broke out between the British and the French, although it wasn't officially declared until 1756. Britain won the French and Indian War (1754–1763) and forced France to give up its claims in North America.

The war cost Britain a lot of money. To help pay for it, Britain placed heavy taxes on English products sold in the colonies, charging more for these goods. Money was scarce, however, and in 1771 a group of farmers in North Carolina formed a group called The Regulators. To protest colonial taxation, they started riots and fired at British troops. Governor Tryon sent more than 1,000 British soldiers to put down the rebellion at the Battle of Alamance Creek. The Regulators were defeated.

North Carolina wasn't the only colony against taxes. Other colonies spoke out, and eventually the taxes were removed from all products except tea. Even the tea tax, however, wasn't acceptable, and protests such as the Boston Tea Party in Massachusetts and the Edenton Tea Party in North Carolina took place. The Edenton Tea Party was organized by a group of North Carolina women who declared that they would drink no more tea, declaring a boycott. This was the first time that American women became involved in politics. Tea was eventually boycotted throughout the colonies.

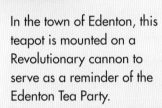

In the town of Edenton, this teapot is mounted on a Revolutionary cannon to serve as a reminder of the Edenton Tea Party.

Resistance to British rule was growing stronger. On May 31, 1775, a group of citizens from Mecklenburg, North Carolina, drew up a document called the Mecklenburg Resolves, declaring freedom from Britain. North Carolina was the first colony to say that it was ready to fight for independence.

North Carolina's official declaration of freedom inspired the other colonies. The desire for freedom was so great that the American Revolutionary War (1775–1783) broke out between Britain and the American colonies. Colonists in North Carolina took opposing sides. The Tories, or Loyalists, wanted British rule. The Whigs, or Patriots, wanted independence. The first battle of the war fought in North Carolina took place on February 2, 1776, at Moore's Creek Bridge.

Meanwhile, representatives from each state had formed a group called the Continental Congress. This group met twice, first in 1774 and again in 1775, when they established the Continental Army headed by George Washington. In 1776 they officially declared independence from Britain by creating a document called the Declaration of Independence. This document stated the reasons why the colonies should be independent of Britain. Two delegates from North Carolina, Joseph Hewes and John Penn, signed the Declaration of Independence on behalf of the state.

A major turning point of the war was the Battle of Guilford Courthouse in Greensboro. Britain won this battle, but their army was terribly weakened—they lost one out of every four soldiers. Seven months later, General Cornwallis, leader of the British troops, surrendered his army at Yorktown, Virginia. The war ended in October 1781, and a peace treaty was signed in 1783.

Once the war was over, plans to create a central government began. Out of these plans was formed the United States Constitution, which established the first system of government. Several states, including North Carolina, feared that the Constitution gave too much power to the federal government. They refused to approve the Federal Constitution without amendments, or changes,

FAMOUS FIRSTS

- North Carolina was the first colony to declare independence from Great Britain
- The first gold rush in the United States started at Reed Gold Mine in 1803
- The University of North Carolina was the first state university in the United States
- The United States opened the first branch of the mint in Charlotte in 1837
- Orville and Wilbur Wright flew the first powered airplane at Kitty Hawk in 1903
- The first protest against segregation took place in Greensboro

General Cornwallis' surrender to General Washington at Yorktown ended the American Revolution.

called the Bill of Rights. When the changes were added, North Carolina signed the Constitution in 1789. North Carolina was the twelfth colony to enter the Union.

THE BEGINNING OF INDEPENDENCE

In the early 1800s, North Carolina had many small farms and a few large plantations. Tobacco and cotton were major crops. The invention of the cotton gin in 1793 increased production of cotton. However, growing the same two crops year after year drained the soil's nutrients. Heavy rains washed away the topsoil, and the damaged soil produced bad crops for many years. Farmers who owned small farms moved out of the state. One out of three people left North Carolina.

In 1835, North Carolina changed its state constitution to allow most male white landowners to vote. After this change, rich plantation owners no longer controlled government. The state legislature voted to develop land for farming in the western part of the state. Another change in the constitution took away the voting rights of free African Americans. This change made a clear division between the two groups.

There was no new economic growth in North Carolina during the first thirty years of the nineteenth century. The government did nothing to help the state grow. As a matter of fact, it seemed as if the state had fallen asleep, like Washington Irving's famous story character, Rip Van Winkle. North Carolina became known as the "Rip Van Winkle State."

By the 1850s the issue of how much power the Union should have over the states came up in North Carolina, along with many other southern states. The northern states opposed slavery. Many people in the southern states wanted to keep slavery. North Carolina was a slave state because it was south of the Mason-Dixon line at the Pennsylvania-Maryland boundary. The Union was split in two.

By 1860 at least 300,000 enslaved African Americans lived in North Carolina. That amounted to one out of three people in the state. However, North Carolina did not have as many slaves as other southern states. Most white people in North Carolina did not own slaves, but they also didn't question slavery as an institution. Slavery was considered essential to the state's agriculture.

North Carolina, however, was one of the original thirteen colonies and, at first, did not want to leave the Union. The turning point came in 1861, when President Abraham Lincoln wanted to put an end to slavery in the South. Many southern states seceded, or separated, from the Union to form the Confederate States of America. President Lincoln

Most of the hard work on southern plantations was done by enslaved African Americans.

asked North Carolina for troops to fight the Confederacy. The North Carolina legislature refused and instead voted to secede from the Union. North Carolina was the last southern state to do so.

At least 125,000 North Carolinians fought in the Confederate Army. One out of every four Southerners killed in the Civil War (1861–1865) was from North Carolina. The state lost nearly 20,000 men in the war, more than any other southern state. Ten important Civil War battles were fought in North Carolina. The bloodiest was at Bentonville, in 1865. This is where North Carolina surrendered its army to the Unionists.

After the war, North Carolina lay in ruins. Towns had been burned and farmland wasted. Between 1867 and 1878, federal troops controlled

Civil War soldiers proudly sent home photographs of themselves to record their participation in the war.

In Berne, North Carolina, people waited in long lines to get clothing during the time of Reconstruction.

North Carolina. This was a time of rebuilding America, called the Reconstruction Era. North Carolina entered the Union again in 1868.

In 1863, Abraham Lincoln had issued the Emancipation Proclamation which declared freedom for all slaves in the South. Former slaves, without money and without homes, wandered from place to place. They began to participate in a free society. For the first time, African Americans could vote. Some even entered politics by joining the Republican Party of Abraham Lincoln.

Members of the Ku Klux Klan burned crosses as a way of terrorizing African Americans.

AFTER THE WAR

In 1868 there was much disagreement about the newly won rights of African Americans. A group of whites called the Ku Klux Klan terrorized African Americans throughout the entire south. "Jim Crow" laws were created that called for segregation, or separation, of white people from African Americans. African-American children were not allowed to attend school with white children. There were separate waiting rooms at bus and train stations. African Americans could not be buried in ground set aside for the burial of white people.

Throughout the Reconstruction Era, North Carolina struggled with a bad economy. Fewer crops were being produced and sold. Many of the

During segregation, a young African-American child is forced to drink out of a water fountain marked "colored."

slaves who had worked in tobacco and cotton fields left the plantations and headed north to find better jobs. Other poor African Americans and poor whites rented land from the planters. But the rents were high, forcing farmers to pay by sharing crops with their landowners. This was called sharecropping.

Until the late 1800s, North Carolina was still a farming state with tobacco and cotton as its main crops. In 1880 three times more cotton was produced than in 1860. To process the cotton, textile mills were started throughout the Piedmont. This industrial development was known as the Cotton Mill Campaign. By the early 1900s, North Carolina's textile mills were the state's chief employer. Towns developed around the mills, and workers lived in houses that were supplied by their employers. Farming was no longer the main industry. Farmers were getting poorer because crop prices were too low and farm expenses were high.

About the same time, a major event took place in North Carolina. Two brothers, Orville and Wilbur Wright, came from Ohio to the North Carolina coast to fly their new invention—a glider with a small engine. In 1903 the Wright brothers flew the first powered flying machine at Kitty Hawk for twelve seconds. This would later provide a new way to travel.

In 1917 the United States entered World War I (1914–1918). More than 86,000 soldiers from North Carolina fought in the war. Army training camps were established around the state. Camp Greene at Charlotte was the largest. Camp Polk was at Raleigh. Both camps were closed after the war. Fort Bragg, near Fayetteville, remained open and would become the largest training center of its kind in the United States.

North Carolinians were hit hard during the Great Depression (1929–1939), a major crisis throughout the United States that caused the value of goods to drop to almost nothing. Poverty touched everywhere across the United States. Farmers lost their farms because they

The Wright Brothers chose Kitty Hawk for their first flight because of its high winds, which averaged 13 miles per hour.

WHO'S WHO IN NORTH CAROLINA?

Josephus Daniels (1862–1948) was the publisher of a major North Carolina newspaper, the *News & Observer*. He also served as Secretary of the Navy (1913–1921) under President Woodrow Wilson.

could not sell their crops. Other people lost their homes and businesses. Eighteen banks in North Carolina were closed. It wasn't until the beginning of World War II (1939–1945) that the country finally began to recover. The United States entered the war in 1941.

Manufactured goods were needed during the war. More jobs were created and people started spending money again. Demand rose again for North Carolina's products. By the 1950s, manufacturing was growing faster in North Carolina than in other states. This continued through the 1970s and the early 1980s. But the country sank into a slump in the 1990s, and North Carolina opened its doors to new, high-tech industries. Soon, these types of industries became even more important than manufacturing in North Carolina.

GROWTH AND CHANGE

Social change was about to happen nationwide. In 1954 the United States Supreme Court ruled that segregating black students from white students in school was against the United States Constitution. North Carolina fought the ruling by agreeing to pay private school tuition for any child "assigned to a public school attended by a child of another race." North Carolina also allowed school districts to close their schools rather than let African Americans attend school with white children. These laws were later overturned.

African Americans began protesting segregation in public places. In 1960, four African-American students sat down at a lunch counter for

After four African-American students were refused service at this Woolworth's lunch counter, many other students filled the chairs for days after, shutting down business.

whites only in an F. W. Woolworth's store in Greensboro. They refused to leave until they were served, coming back day after day. The action of these students set off a similar chain of protests across the South. Three years later, Congress passed the Civil Rights Act of 1964. This act desegregated all public places by law. By the 1970s whites and African Americans were attending public school together in North Carolina.

EXTRA! EXTRA!

Today, the Greensboro Woolworth's is closed. In 1993, two of the original four protestors bought the store, and had plans to reopen it as "The International Civil Rights Center and Museum." There was some controversy over the project and it has since come to a standstill. A section of the Woolworth's counter and newsclips are now on display at the National Museum of American History in Washington, D.C.

Throughout the 1960s and 1970s, the state began spending more money on public schools. Interest in books, art, and music grew.

In 1985 North Carolina created the Basic Education Program by developing better study programs for students. Now there are more than 1,500 elementary schools and 300 secondary schools in the state. North Carolina also has many private schools, some of which are run by churches. The Carolina Agency for Jewish Education offers educational programs to both Jewish and non-Jewish North Carolinians.

Duke University, in Durham, was founded in 1924.

Many colleges and universities are located throughout the state. The University of North Carolina has sixteen schools in various cities, including Chapel Hill and Charlotte. Duke University in Durham is one of the best in the United States. Salem College was the first privately run college in North Carolina and one of the first women's colleges in the United States. The state also has 58 community colleges.

But while North Carolina was working to improve the state, many people moved out. They went to northern cities to look for better-paying jobs. To bring business back, North Carolina lowered taxes. In 1961 the state created a 5,000-acre (2,000-hectare) research park located in the middle of Chapel Hill, Durham, and Raleigh. (If you look on a map you'll see that these three cities can be connected with a triangle.) Through the years, Research Triangle Park grew to 7,000 acres (2,832 hectares). As a result, people started returning to the state by the 1980s. Today, the Park has 140 organizations employing 44,000 people. North Carolina is a booming state.

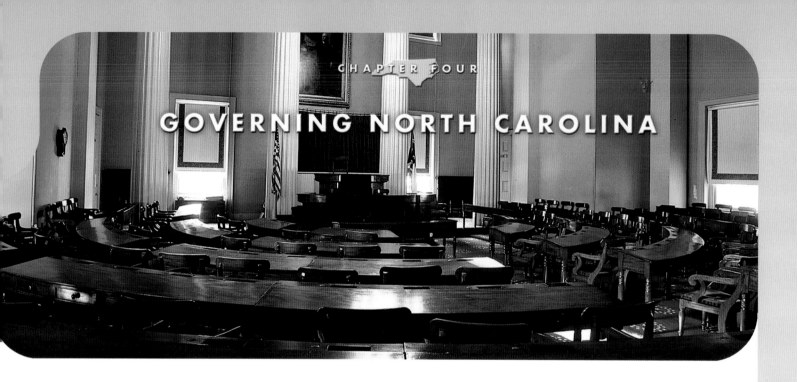

CHAPTER FOUR

GOVERNING NORTH CAROLINA

The historic House chamber is at the state capitol in Raleigh.

North Carolinians have always been independent. North Carolina was one of the original thirteen colonies, and it was the first colony to vote for independence from Great Britain. North Carolinians defined the basic principles by which it would govern its people in a document known as the constitution, adopted in 1776. In 1868 they wrote a second constitution that was later amended, or changed, thirty times to create laws of segregation, and to take away voting power from African Americans. In 1971 North Carolina wrote a third constitution. It declared that "all elections shall be free" and that the state would not treat one group of people better than another because of race, color, or religion. This constitution is still used today.

The state government of North Carolina is similar to the federal government of the United States. Both governments have three branches—the executive, the legislative, and the judicial. Together,

This statue in Raleigh commemorates three presidents who were born in North Carolina—Andrew Jackson, Andrew Johnson, and James Polk.

these branches of government make and carry out laws that protect the welfare of all citizens.

THE EXECUTIVE BRANCH

The executive branch enforces the state's laws. North Carolina's governor is head of the executive branch. He or she is elected for a four-year term by the people of North Carolina, and can only be elected twice.

WHO'S WHO IN NORTH CAROLINA?

Terry Sanford (1917–1998). This former governor of North Carolina was born in Laurinburg. He was president of Duke University and also a United States senator.

The governor has several duties. One of the most important is planning the state's budget. The budget shows how much money the state can spend on services for its citizens. The governor can also propose laws or veto (say no to) laws that the legislature passed. The governor is also the commander-in-chief of the state's military forces and can call out the militia to protect North Carolina's citizens if necessary.

THE LEGISLATIVE BRANCH

The legislative branch of government makes new laws. North Carolina laws may focus on building schools and other public buildings and highways. Paying for health care and reducing crime are other problems that come before the legislature. The legislature also studies the budget recommended by the governor and decides how much money the state will pay to educate, protect, and help its citizens.

WHO'S WHO IN NORTH CAROLINA?

Senator Jesse Helms (1921–) was born in Monroe. He served five terms in the U.S. Senate between 1973 and 2003. He is the first North Carolinian to receive the Golden Gavel for presiding over the Senate more than 117 hours in 1973, and more than 120 hours in 1974.

The legislative building in Raleigh includes both the Senate and House Chambers.

The capitol building in Raleigh replaced the old state house, which burned down in 1831.

The members of the legislative branch are called the General Assembly. They meet once a year at the Legislative Building in Raleigh. The General Assembly is made up of two groups—the House of Representatives and the Senate. The House of Representatives has 120 members, and the Senate has 50 members. Each member of the legislature is elected to serve for two years.

THE JUDICIAL BRANCH

The judicial branch is the state's court system, which interprets the laws. In a dispute, the courts hear both sides of a case to decide whether or not laws have been broken. The courts also decide on the penalty.

NORTH CAROLINA STATE GOVERNMENT

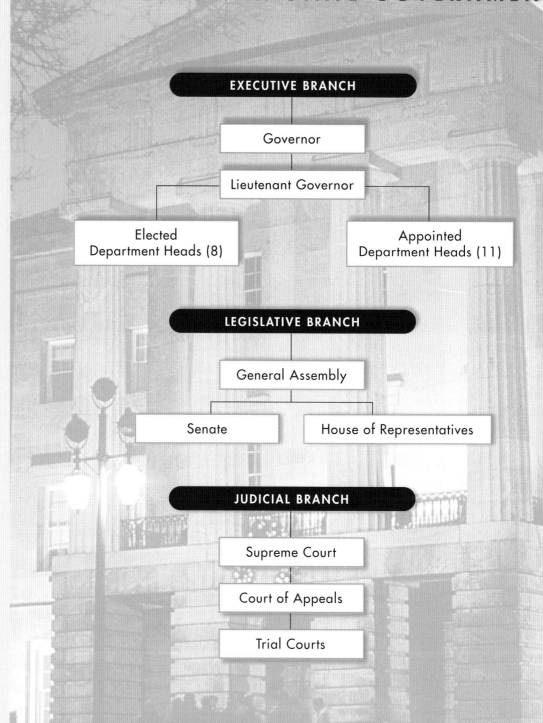

EXECUTIVE BRANCH

Governor

Lieutenant Governor

Elected
Department Heads (8)

Appointed
Department Heads (11)

LEGISLATIVE BRANCH

General Assembly

Senate

House of Representatives

JUDICIAL BRANCH

Supreme Court

Court of Appeals

Trial Courts

NORTH CAROLINA GOVERNORS

Name	Term	Name	Term
Richard Caswell	1776–1780	Z.B. Vance	1862–1865
Abner Nash	1780–1781	W.W. Holden (provisional governor)	1865
Thomas Burke	1781–1782	Jonathan Worth	1865–1868
Alexander Martin	1782–1784	W.W. Holden	1868–1871
Richard Caswell	1784–1787	T.R. Caldwell	1871–1874
Samuel Johnston	1787–1789	C.H. Brogden	1874–1877
Alexander Martin	1789–1792	Z.B. Vance	1877–1879
R.D. Spaight Sr.	1792–1795	T.J. Jarvis	1879–1885
Samuel Ashe	1795–1798	A.M. Scalees	1885–1889
W.R. Davie	1798–1799	D.G. Fowle	1889–1891
Benjamin Williams	1799–1802	Thomas M. Holt	1891–1893
James Turner	1802–1805	Elias Carr	1893–1897
Nathaniel Alexander	1805–1807	D.L. Russell	1897–1901
Benjamin Williams	1807–1808	Charles B. Aycock	1901–1905
David Stone	1808–1810	R.B. Glenn	1905–1909
Benjamin Smith	1810–1811	W.W. Kitchin	1909–1913
William Hawkins	1811–1814	Locke Craig	1913–1917
William Miller	1814–1817	Thomas W. Bickett	1917–1921
John Branch	1817–1820	Cameron Morrison	1921–1925
Jesse Franklin	1820–1821	Angus Wilton McLean	1925–1929
Gabriel Holmes	1821–1824	O. Max Gardner	1929–1933
H.G. Burton	1824–1827	J.C.B. Ehringhaus	1933–1937
James Iredell Jr.	1827–1828	Clyde R. Hoey	1937–1941
John Owen	1828–1830	J. Melville Broughton	1941–1945
Montfort Stokes	1830–1832	R. Gregg Cherry	1945–1949
D.L. Swain	1832–1835	W. Kerr Scott	1949–1953
R.D. Spaight Jr.	1835–1836	William B. Umstead	1953–1954
E.B. Dudley	1836–1841	Luther H. Hodges	1954–1961
J.M. Morehead	1841–1845	Terry Sanford	1961–1965
W.A. Graham	1845–1849	Daniel K. Moore	1965–1969
Charles Manly	1849–1851	Robert W. Scott	1969–1973
D.S. Reid	1851–1854	James E. Holshouser Jr.	1973–1977
Warren Winslow	1854–1855	James B. Hunt Jr.	1977–1985
Thomas Bragg	1855–1859	James G. Martin	1985–1993
John W. Ellis	1859–1861	James B. Hunt Jr.	1993–2001
Henry T. Clark	1861–1862	Michael F. Easley	2001–2008

Raleigh is a booming city with many new people and businesses moving in each year.

District courts hear civil cases that involve less than $10,000 and don't involve a crime. Civil cases are disputes that may involve unlawful activities, such as a dispute between a group of citizens and a city about the use of a public building. District courts also handle cases involving young people.

At the next level, the Court of Appeals reviews cases ruled on by the lower courts and determines whether or not the correct decision was made. The Court of Appeals may overturn (reverse) or uphold the lower court's decision. There are twelve judges in the Court of Appeals.

If the court upholds the lower ruling, the case may be appealed to the state Supreme Court, the state's highest court. A chief justice and six justices preside over the state Supreme Court. The decision of this court is final.

All North Carolina judges are elected. District judges serve a term of four years. Other justices and judges serve eight years.

TAKE A TOUR OF RALEIGH, THE STATE CAPITAL

Raleigh is known as the "City of Oaks" because it has many trees and parks. It is one of the fastest growing cities in the United States—more than 280,000 people live here! Many scientists and businesspeople have come from all over the world to work at nearby Research Triangle Park.

Raleigh is laid out in a grid pattern with the capitol building in the center. The capitol was built in 1840. Today it is a national historic

Raleigh is a mix of old and new. The Oakwood Historic District has many old homes dating back to the nineteenth century.

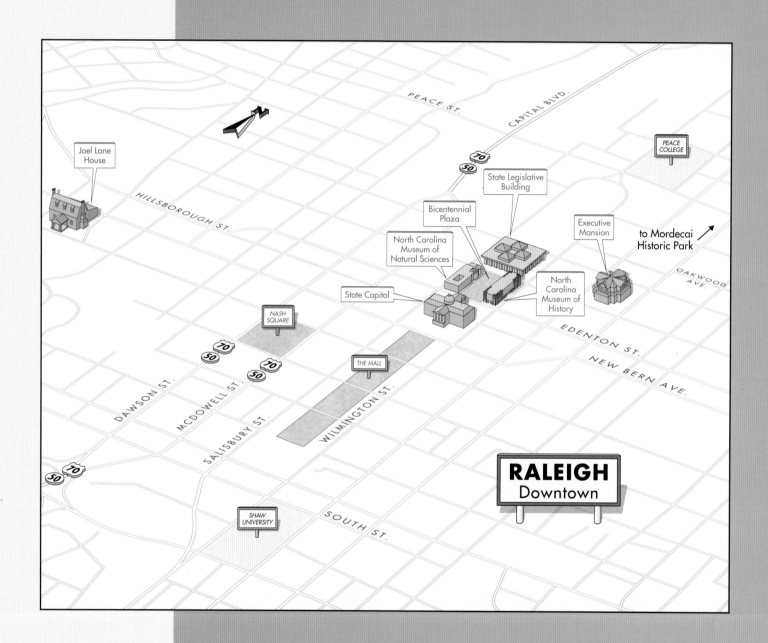

Joel Lane
House

PEACE ST.

CAPITAL BLVD.

PEACE
COLLEGE

State Legislative
Building

Bicentennial
Plaza

HILLSBOROUGH ST.

Executive
Mansion

to Mordecai
Historic Park

North Carolina
Museum of
Natural Sciences

OAKWOOD AVE.

State Capitol

North
Carolina
Museum of
History

EDENTON ST.

NASH
SQUARE

NEW BERN AVE.

THE MALL

DAWSON ST.

MCDOWELL ST.

SALISBURY ST.

WILMINGTON ST.

RALEIGH
Downtown

SHAW
UNIVERSITY

SOUTH ST.

landmark. The building is shaped like a cross with a copper dome rising ten stories above it. Under the dome is a life-size statue of George Washington dressed like a Roman general. At one time, all government offices were located in the capitol, but today only the executive offices, including the governor's office, are here.

If you walk one block north of the capitol you'll find the State Legislative Building. When the General Assembly is in session, you can watch lawmakers in action from the gallery upstairs.

Close by is the Oakwood Historic District. This section of the city has more than 400 private homes, all built in the 1800s. The oldest

North Carolina's Executive Mansion is listed on the National Register of Historic Places. It was built in 1891.

home in Raleigh is the Wakefield, or Joel Lane House. Built in 1760, it was named for Margaret Wake, the wife of a royal governor. Colonel Joel Lane, the "father of Raleigh," lived in the house. In 1792 he sold 1,000 acres (400 hectares) of land to the state for its capital. Today, the governor and his family live in the Executive Mansion, not far away from the Oakwood Historic District.

Andrew Johnson, the seventeenth president of the United States (1865–1869), was born in Raleigh in 1808. You can visit his birthplace on Village Street in Mordecai Historic Park.

Another stop on the tour is the African American Cultural Complex, where you'll learn about the history of African Americans. Three cottages are filled with exhibits, an outdoor stage, and nature trails. On display are African masks, inventions of African Americans (such as a saddle invented by African-American cowboys), and exhibits about well-known African-American women. Forty thousand people a year visit this museum and educational center.

You'll need plenty of time to tour the next stop—the North Carolina Museum of Natural Sciences. It is the largest natural history museum in the southeast. You'll learn all about the natural world through exhibits like Mountains to the Sea, which recreates five North Carolina habitats, complete with live animals and waterfalls. You can also see a fossilized dinosaur heart, and whale skeletons of coastal Carolina. If you prefer getting your hands dirty, check out the interactive exhibits, where you can examine objects through microscopes, listen to the ocean in a sea shell, and touch fossils, rocks, and even bird wings.

Andrew Johnson was the seventeenth United States president. He took over after Abraham Lincoln's death.

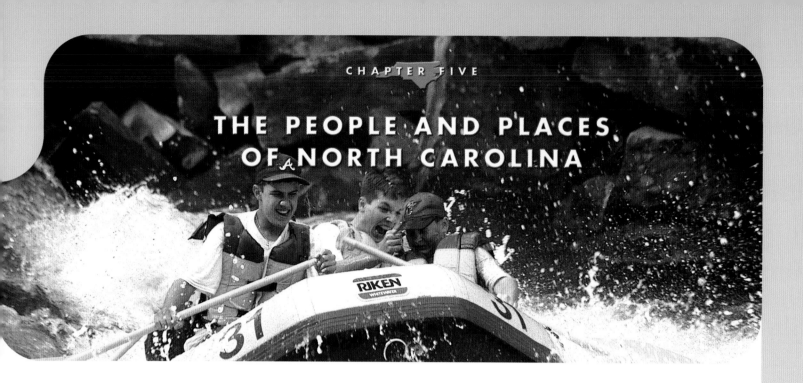

CHAPTER FIVE

THE PEOPLE AND PLACES OF NORTH CAROLINA

The Nantahala River is a popular place for whitewater rafting.

North Carolina ranks twenty-ninth in size compared to other states. But a lot of people live here—so many, in fact, that North Carolina is the eleventh most populated state! Many different races and ethnic backgrounds are represented by its people.

MEET THE PEOPLE

According to the 2000 Census, more than eight million people live in the Tar Heel State. North Carolina is one of the fastest-growing states in the country. About 72 out of every 100 people are of European descent. African Americans make up the second largest group, with 22 out of every 100 people. The number of Asians and Hispanics took a big jump in the 1990s. About seven out of 100 people are either Hispanic or Native American, and almost two out of 100 people are Asian.

A diversity of races is represented in North Carolina's schools.

In the last ten years, people have been steadily spilling out of North Carolina's big cities and into the mountains and coastal areas. Nearly half of all North Carolinians live in small towns and rural areas. North Carolinians are country folks at heart. Country cooking is popular—everything from grits to fried catfish and sweet potato pie.

Many North Carolinians prefer to live in rural areas and small towns like Waynesville.

Still, some people have left farm life for city life. Charlotte is the largest city in North Carolina. The other six urban centers are in the Piedmont region and can be grouped into two geographical areas: the Triad and the Triangle. The state capital, Raleigh, along with Durham and Chapel Hill—two major university towns—form the Triangle. Research Triangle Park is in the center.

The Triad is made up of Greensboro, Winston-Salem, and High Point. Greensboro and Winston-Salem have historic importance. At the Battle of Guilford Courthouse in 1781, one out of four British soldiers was killed or wounded. This weakened the British troops and helped the Americans win the Revolutionary War. The site of the first settlement of Moravians, a religious group from Germany, is in Winston-Salem. High Point is the "Home Furnishings Capital of the World" with over 125 furniture factories.

Tours are conducted at many of North Carolina's furniture factories.

NORTH CAROLINA RECIPE

Hush puppies are a popular side dish from North Carolina. When you finish making this recipe, you'll have a lot of corny "pups!" Remember, get a grown-up to help you.

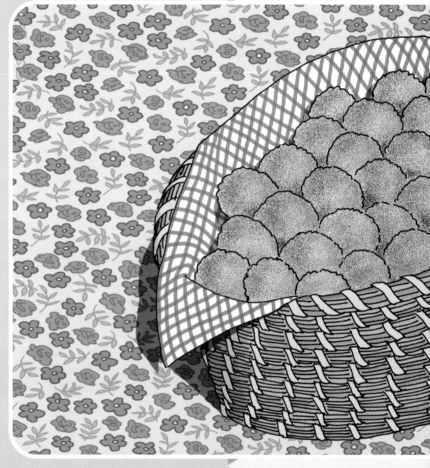

HUSH PUPPIES

2 cups yellow cornmeal
1 cup plain flour
2 eggs
1 cup buttermilk (or substitute regular milk)
3/4 teaspoon seasoned salt
1/2 teaspoon ground pepper blend
1 teaspoon baking powder
2/3 teaspoon baking soda
1/8 cup low-fat cooking oil

1. Fill a frying pan half full with cooking oil. Heat over medium-high heat.
2. Mix the cornmeal, flour, seasoned salt, pepper, baking powder, and baking soda in a bowl.
3. Add the eggs, oil, and buttermilk. Stir until blended.
4. Using a tablespoon, drop the batter into the frying pan.
5. Brown them on all sides. The hush puppies will float when done. Do not overcook.

WORKING IN NORTH CAROLINA

In the early days, most North Carolinians were farmers. They lived off the crops of the land—tobacco and cotton. In 1960 North Carolina had about 212,000 farms. Now there are about 48,000 farms, but agriculture is still the state's number one industry. Almost 22 out of every 100 people work in farming. North Carolina's farmers produce more tobacco and sweet potatoes than any other state. Other farmers raise hogs and cattle. North Carolina's farmers produce crops and livestock worth about $40 billion a year.

Tobacco is still one of North Carolina's most important crops.

Many of North Carolina's service jobs are in sales, insurance, and real estate. Service workers also sell textiles, tobacco products, and furniture. Textile producers built factories in North Carolina and elsewhere in the South because wages are relatively low. One out of every three other service workers in North Carolina are doctors and nurses, lawyers, teachers, insurance salespeople, repair technicians, and government employees.

High-tech industry has created a lot of jobs in North Carolina. Thousands of scientists, engineers, and computer technicians work in the research divisions of major corporations at Research Triangle Park west of Raleigh. It is the largest research park in the United States. Many people are also employed by banks. In the 1980s, Charlotte developed into a major banking center, and today the state ranks second in the nation in the banking industry.

About one out of every three people in North Carolina work in manufacturing. As many as 900,000 people work in factories. The value of their products is nearly $60 billion a year. After North Carolina's first

Many people who live in the "triangle"—Raleigh, Chapel Hill, and Durham—are employed at Research Triangle Park.

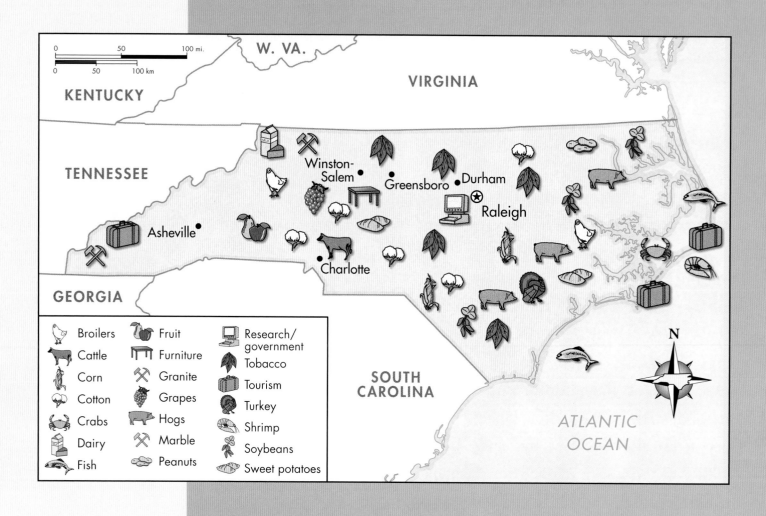

KENTUCKY

W. VA.

VIRGINIA

TENNESSEE

Winston-Salem

Greensboro

Durham

Raleigh

Asheville

Charlotte

GEORGIA

SOUTH CAROLINA

ATLANTIC OCEAN

N

	Broilers		Fruit		Research/government
	Cattle		Furniture		Tobacco
	Corn		Granite		Tourism
	Cotton		Grapes		Turkey
	Crabs		Hogs		Shrimp
	Dairy		Marble		Soybeans
	Fish		Peanuts		Sweet potatoes

0   50   100 mi.
0   50   100 km

cotton mill was built in 1813, textiles became the main industry. Today, 2,100 textile plants produce sheets, towels, denim, and other items.

The fishing and seafood industry brings in about $65 million. Morehead City and Beaufort are major fishing ports in the state. Morehead City hosts a Seafood Festival every year to educate the public about seafood and its importance to the state's economy. The Festival also recognizes the many men and women who work in the fishing industry. North Carolina is careful to protect its waters from overfishing, a problem that occurred in the mid-1990s. Today, the harvesting of fish is controlled so that the people of North Carolina—and the rest of the country—will continually have fish for sale in their grocery stores.

Tourism is also a big industry in North Carolina. Every year, tourists spend about $10 billion visiting North Carolina's famous sites and recreation areas of national and state parks. The travel industry is as important as manufacturing and agriculture in North Carolina.

TAKING A TOUR OF NORTH CAROLINA

Eastern North Carolina and the Outer Banks

Beaches line the coast of North Carolina. The Cape Hatteras National Seashore alone stretches 72 miles (116 km). It was the first national seashore in the United States. A short ferry ride will take you to Cape Lookout National Seashore, which extends 55 miles (89 km).

There are many historic sites to visit all along the coast. The story of the Lost Colony on Roanoke Island is told through an outdoor play

The Historic Jones House, built in 1808, is in New Bern's historic district.

every night at the Fort Raleigh National Historic Site in Manteo. Fort Raleigh is where Sir Walter Raleigh tried to start an English settlement. The Wright Brothers National Memorial to the first powered airplane flight is at Kill Devil Hill. (You can't miss it because it looks like the tail of an airplane.) Fort Fisher and Fort Macon are worth seeing, too. Both forts fell to Union armies during the Civil War. Then, travel on to Ocracoke Island to see the port where Blackbeard hid to plan his attack on ships from Europe.

Several coastal towns, like Bath and New Bern, have historic districts. The buildings in these districts look the same as they did in the 1700s. St. Thomas Episcopal Church, the oldest church in the state, is located in Bath. New Bern was the colony's first capital. The largest historic district is in Wilmington. It covers 200 blocks. You can take a carriage ride to see the old homes and gardens, or cruise on the river. The battleship *North Carolina* is docked just beyond the downtown area. This ship was used in every major naval attack in the Pacific Ocean during World War II.

Central North Carolina

Most of North Carolina's cities are in the Piedmont, or central North Carolina. More than 500,000 people live in Charlotte, the largest city in the state. As a matter of fact, it was the second fastest-growing city of its size in the last ten years. At 174.3 square miles (451 sq km), Charlotte is a big presence in the state. Even the top of the 60-story Bank of America Corporate Center looks like a crown.

Lowe's Motor Speedway in Charlotte is used for stock car racing.

Charlotte is laid out in four wards, or sections, around Independence Square. The Fourth Ward has eighteen sites that are hundreds of years old, including the Old Settlers Cemetery behind the First Presbyterian Church. Some tombstones date from the 1700s. Discovery Place, the city's main attraction, is near Fourth Ward Park. Visitors can see the science museum, aquariums, and even a rain forest with exotic birds and waterfalls. The biggest planetarium in the United States is also in a theater here. After Discovery Place, stop by Wing Haven Gardens and Bird Sanctuary. You'll find more than 135 kinds of birds here, including warblers and mockingbirds.

For basketball fans, Charlotte is home to the Bobcats, an NBA team that was founded in 2004. The Carolina Panthers football team plays at Bank of America Stadium.

There's a lot to see just a short drive from Charlotte, too. The Reed Gold Mine in Stanfield was the first gold mine in the United States. Twelve-year-old Conrad Reed found gold on his family farm here. His discovery set off the first gold rush in the country. About ten miles (16 km) south of Charlotte is a large theme park called Carowinds.

Fans crowd into Charlotte Bobcats Arena to watch their team play basketball.

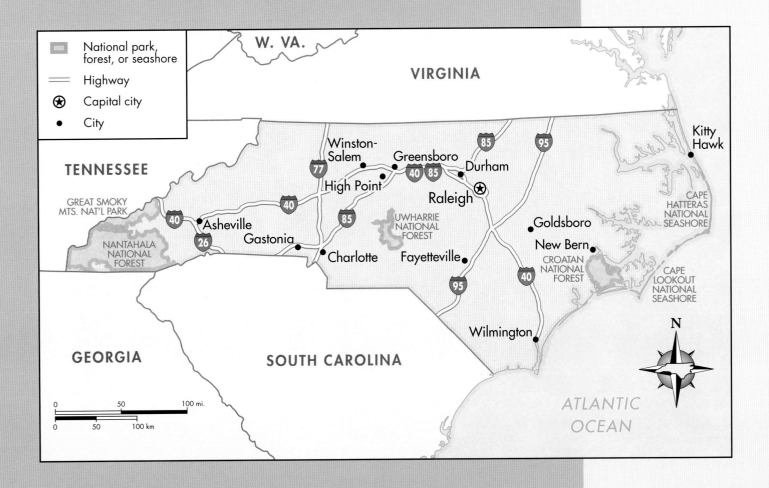

W. VA.

VIRGINIA

National park, forest, or seashore

Highway

Capital city

City

TENNESSEE

GREAT SMOKY
MTS. NAT'L PARK

NANTAHALA
NATIONAL
FOREST

Winston-
Salem

High Point

Greensboro

Durham

Raleigh

Asheville

Gastonia

Charlotte

UWHARRIE
NATIONAL
FOREST

Fayetteville

Goldsboro

New Bern

CROATAN
NATIONAL
FOREST

Kitty
Hawk

CAPE
HATTERAS
NATIONAL
SEASHORE

CAPE
LOOKOUT
NATIONAL
SEASHORE

Wilmington

GEORGIA

SOUTH CAROLINA

**ATLANTIC
OCEAN**

N

0   50   100 mi.

0   50   100 km

Take a time-out at
Carowinds theme park!

Take a roller coaster ride standing up on Vortex, or hunt ghosts and collect Scooby snacks in Scooby Doo's haunted mansion. The park also sponsors Education Days, where you can learn about science, math, and more through workshops, demonstrations, and exhibits.

The North Carolina Zoological Park is near Asheboro. It is the country's largest walk-through natural habitat zoo, where the animals and plants are shown in their natural settings. Five miles of trails wind through the Uwharrie Mountains where you'll see gorillas, giraffes, polar bears, tropical birds, and many other animals.

At the North Carolina Zoological Park you can see all kinds of animals in their natural environment.

Other attractions in central North Carolina include the Sandhills in the southeast. It is a popular golf resort, and the area also has a number of peach orchards. About eight miles (13 km) east of Greensboro is the Charlotte Hawkins Brown Memorial State Historic Site. It is located on the campus of a high school for African Americans. Dr. Charlotte Hawkins Brown ran the school for fifty years.

Western North Carolina

The mountains of North Carolina attract visitors year-round. In the Black Mountains, you can climb Mount Mitchell, the highest peak in the eastern United States. Great Smoky Mountain National Park and other state parks have campsites and hiking trails. You can also visit their craft shops.

The northern mountain region of the state is called the High Country. The town of Blowing Rock in the Blue Ridge Mountains got its name for a good reason. If you toss a lightweight object over the 4,000-foot (1,220-m) cliff at the Johns River Gorge, it may come flying right back to you! Even snow appears to fall upside down. Nearby is Tweetsie Railroad, a railroad that dates back to 1866. If you take a ride on the Tweetsie today you'll see lots of beautiful scenery—but you may also have to

This building is at the top of Mount Mitchell, the highest peak east of the Mississippi.

opposite:
This 250-room house was built for 26-year-old multimillionaire George W. Vanderbilt. Today it is one of North Carolina's most popular tourist sites.

fight off train robbers from the old Wild West!

Asheville is the largest city in the mountains. About 63,000 people live here, including many artists and craftspeople. The Penland School of Crafts is located 45 miles (72 km) northeast of Asheville. It is the oldest and largest arts and crafts school of its kind in North America. Also in Asheville is the Park Place Education, Arts & Science Center, where you can visit several museums and go to the theater all in one spot.

The Biltmore estate, home of George Vanderbilt, is also in Asheville. Vanderbilt was one of the wealthiest men in the United States. With 250 rooms, the Biltmore Estate is the largest private residence in the nation. Some of Vanderbilt's relatives still live here. In 1996 the North Carolina Arboretum opened gardens on part of the estate, with flowers planted in patterns. The Quilt Garden is arranged in the pattern of a country quilt. It took

ten years to create these complex flower gardens.

South of Asheville in the Highlands is Bridal Veil Falls—a drive-through waterfall! When the road was first built decades ago, drivers had no choice but to steer behind the waterfall. Today, it's not necessary to drive through the falls unless you want to. The falls drop 120 feet (37 m) over the road.

Southeast of Asheville is Chimney Rock Park, the site of a giant rock that offers incredible views. You can take an elevator up 26 stories to the top, or, if you're feeling adventurous, you can walk up stairs through narrow passageways and explore caves and forests along your way to the Rock. Some places within the park were shown in the film "The Last of the Mohicans." At certain times of the year, professional rope and rock climbers do demonstrations on different rock faces throughout the park.

To the west of Asheville is the town of Cherokee. Cherokee is in the Qualla

Boundary—part of 56,000 acres (22,400 hectares) of reservation land for the Eastern Cherokee tribe. In 1838 the United States government forced the Cherokees to leave their homes in North Carolina and go to Oklahoma. Many Cherokees refused. Although some of them hid in the mountains, most of the Cherokees were forced out of their homes. About 4,000 Cherokees died on their travels west, known as the "Trail of Tears." By 1866, the Cherokees who stayed in North Carolina were given back their homeland. Six hundred Cherokees live in the town of Cherokee. More than 8,000 other members of the tribe live in communities within the Qualla Boundary.

opposite:
This photo shows a Cherokee man in traditional dress.

NORTH CAROLINA ALMANAC

Statehood date and number: November 21, 1789; 12th state

State seal: Adopted 1984

State flag: Adopted 1885

Geographic center: In Chatham County 35º 42N 79º 16W

Total area/rank: 53,819 square miles (139,389 sq km)/29th

Coastline: approximately 320 miles (515 km)

Borders: Virginia, Tennessee, South Carolina, Georgia, Atlantic Ocean

Latitude and longitude: North Carolina is located approximately between 33° 52' and 36° 34' N and 75° 27' and 84° 20'W

Highest/lowest elevation: Mount Mitchell, 6,684 feet (2,037 m)/Atlantic Coast, sea level

Hottest/coldest temperature: 110°F (43°C) at Fayetteville on August 21, 1983/–34°F (–51°C) at Mount Mitchell on January 21, 1985

Land area/rank: 48,711 square miles (126,161 sq km)/29th

Inland water area: 3,960 square miles (10,256 sq km)

Population/rank: 8,049,313 (2000 Census)/11th

Population of major cities:
Charlotte: 540,828
Raleigh: 276,093
Greensboro: 223,891
Durham: 187,035
Winston-Salem: 185,776

Origin of state name: Carolus, named after King Charles

State capital: Raleigh

Previous capitals: New Bern

Counties: 100

State government: 50 senators, 120 representatives

Major rivers, lakes: Roanoke, Tar-Pamlico, Neuse, Cape Fear; Lake Waccamaw, Lake Mattamuskeet

Farm products: Cotton, tobacco, soybeans, corn, food grains, wheat, peanuts, sweet potatoes

Livestock: Cattle/calves, hogs/pigs, and chickens

Manufactured products: Food products, tobacco products, chemicals, furniture, paper, apparel, mica, lithium, industrial machinery, and electrical and electronic equipment

Mining products: Crushed stone, phosphate rock, sand, and gravel clays

Fishing products: Drum, bluefish, mackerel, flounder, tarpon, tuna, pompano, gray trout, whiting, croaker, spots, mullet, spotted sea trout, bass, and catfish

Beverage: Milk

Bird: Cardinal

Boat: Shad boat

Colors: Red and blue

Dog: Plott hound

Fair: Raleigh

Flower: Dogwood

Gem: Emerald

Insect: Honeybee

Mammal: Gray squirrel

Motto: Esse quam videri (To be, rather than to seem)

Nicknames: Tar Heel State, Old North State

Reptile: Eastern box turtle

Rock: Granite

Saltwater fish: Channel bass

Shell: Scotch bonnet

Song: "The Old North State"

Toast: Tar heel toast

Tree: Pine

Vegetable: Sweet potato

Wildlife: Deer, foxes, rabbits, squirrels, groundhogs, black bears, bobcats, red wolves, European wild boar, otters, minks, muskrats, beavers, alligators, turtles, coral snakes, copperhead snakes, cottonmouth water moccasins, rattlesnakes, salamanders

TIME**LINE**

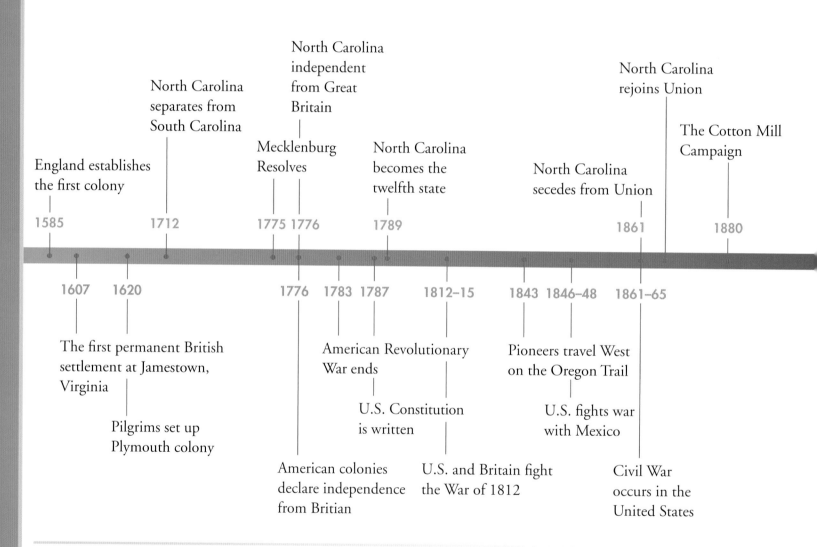

North Carolina independent from Great Britain

North Carolina rejoins Union

North Carolina separates from South Carolina

The Cotton Mill Campaign

Mecklenburg Resolves

North Carolina becomes the twelfth state

North Carolina secedes from Union

England establishes the first colony

| 1585 | 1712 | 1775 | 1776 | 1789 | 1861 | 1880 |

| 1607 | 1620 | 1776 | 1783 | 1787 | 1812–15 | 1843 | 1846–48 | 1861–65 |

The first permanent British settlement at Jamestown, Virginia

American Revolutionary War ends

Pioneers travel West on the Oregon Trail

Pilgrims set up Plymouth colony

U.S. Constitution is written

U.S. fights war with Mexico

American colonies declare independence from Britian

U.S. and Britain fight the War of 1812

Civil War occurs in the United States

UNITED STATES **HISTORY**

72

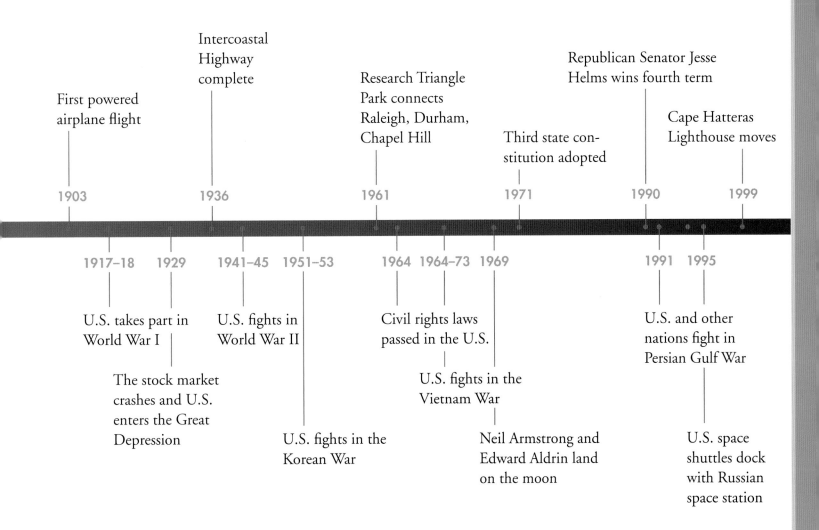

Intercoastal
Highway
complete

First powered
airplane flight

Research Triangle
Park connects
Raleigh, Durham,
Chapel Hill

Republican Senator Jesse
Helms wins fourth term

Third state con-
stitution adopted

Cape Hatteras
Lighthouse moves

1903   1936   1961   1971   1990   1999

1917–18   1929   1941–45   1951–53   1964   1964–73   1969   1991   1995

U.S. takes part in
World War I

U.S. fights in
World War II

Civil rights laws
passed in the U.S.

U.S. and other
nations fight in
Persian Gulf War

The stock market
crashes and U.S.
enters the Great
Depression

U.S. fights in the
Vietnam War

U.S. fights in the
Korean War

Neil Armstrong and
Edward Aldrin land
on the moon

U.S. space
shuttles dock
with Russian
space station

GALLERY OF FAMOUS NORTH CAROLINIANS

Curtis L. Brown, Jr.
(1956–)
Astronaut and colonel in the United States Air Force. Born in Elizabethtown.

Virginia Dare
(1587–?)
First child born in the new world to English parents.

Elizabeth Hanford Dole
(1936–)
Former president of the Red Cross. Campaigned for president of the United States in 1999. Born in Salisbury.

James Buchanan Duke
(1856–1925)
President of the American Tobacco Company in 1890. Born in Durham.

Billy Graham
(1918–)
Well-known evangelist. Born in Charlotte.

Andy Griffith
(1926–)
Television actor in series such as *The Andy Griffith Show* and *Matlock*. Born in Mount Airy.

Jesse Helms
(1921–)
Reelected five times to United States Senate, representing North Carolina.

Jim "Catfish" Hunter
(1946–1999)
All-Star baseball pitcher. Born in Hertford.

Andrew Johnson
(1808–1875)
Seventeenth president of the United States. Born in Raleigh.

Hiram Rhoades Revels
(1822–1901)
First African-American member of Congress. Elected U.S. senator in 1870. Born in Fayetteville.

GLOSSARY

amendment: a change made to a main legal document

charter: a government paper that allows certain people to rule

colonization: the act of founding a colony

colony: a settlement located outside of a parent country but ruled by the same country

Confederacy: The Confederate States of America organized after several southern states broke away from the Union when the Civil War started

delegates: people who are elected to represent a state or a country

economy: the growth of a country measured in dollars

expedition: a trip made by a group of people with a certain purpose

explorers: people who travel to unknown lands to find out about them

hurricane: a storm that develops over the ocean

independence: freedom from the control of government

industry: the manufacture of a product

legislature: a government body that makes laws

meteor: a small, fiery mass of stone that travels from outer space into the earth's atmosphere

plantation: a very large farm in the South

population: the number of people who live in a place

prehistoric: before history was written

segregation: a practice in which people may be separated according to race, color, or religion

settlers: people who move into a new area where nobody else has lived

territory: a region that belongs to a state or a foreign country

unconstitutional: against the principles of the state or federal constitution

FOR MORE INFORMATION

Web sites

North Carolina
http://www.visitnc.com
Provides tourist information.

Welcome to North Carolina
http://www.ncgov.com
Official web site for the North Carolina state government.

State Library of North Carolina
http://statelibrary.dcr.state.nc.us/NCSLHOME.HTM
Connects users to information about North Carolina history and government.

Secretary of State Kids' Page
http://www.secretary.state.nc.us/kidspg/homepage.asp
Provides fun facts about North Carolina.

Carolina Clips
http://www.itpi.dpi.state.nc.us/caroclips/default.html
Information about North Carolina, developed by the NC Department of Public Instruction.

Books

Fleischner, Jennifer. *I Was Born a Slave: The Story of Harriet Jacobs.* Brookfield, CT: Millbrook Press, 2000.

Hintz, Martin and Stephen Hintz. *North Carolina.* New York: Children's Press, 1998.

Kent, Zachary. *Andrew Johnson (Encyclopedia of Presidents).* Danbury, CT: Children's Press, 1989.

Tillage, Leon. *Leon's Story.* New York, NY: Farrar Straus Giroux, 1997.

Weatherford, Carole Boston. *Sink or Swim: African-American Lifesavers of the Outer Banks.* Carolina Press, 1999.

Addresses

North Carolina Department of Cultural Resources
109 East Jones Street
MSC 4604
Raleigh, NC 27699-4604

North Carolina Division of Tourism, Film and Sports Development
301 N. Wilmington Street
Raleigh, NC 27601

INDEX

ABOUT THE AUTHOR

Nancy Axelrad, who writes under the pen name Nan Alex, was part of the original team that produced dozens of popular books including *Nancy Drew*, the *Hardy Boys*, and the *Bobbsey Twins*. Nancy authored a number of the books and has written many magazine stories and articles for children.

Long before Nancy wrote *North Carolina*, she visited the state. To write this book, Nancy talked to a number of native North Carolinians, used the Internet, and read many books about the state.

Photographs ©2008: AP Images/Dave Martin: 17; Corbis Images: 20 (Bettmann), 14 (David Muench); Ernest H. Robl: 40 right; Getty Images: 27, 49 (Archive Photos), 74 top right (Ken Cedeno), 12 top, 54 (Richard A. Cooke III), 7 (Wayne Eastep), 60 (Elsa), 24, 29, 36 left (Hulton Getty), 59 (Craig Jones), 40 left (Bob Padgett), 44 (Donovan Reese), 74 left (Sporting News); Library of Congress: 32; MapQuest.com, Inc.: 70; NASA: 74 bottom right; North Carolina Department of Cultural Resources, Division of Archives & History: 23, 30 left; North Carolina Division of Tourism, Film and Sports Development: 41, 42, 52; North Carolina Museum of Natural Sciences: 48; Photo Researchers, NY: 71 bottom left (Stephen Dalton), 39 (Frederica Georgia), 13 (Jeff Lepore), 33 (Library of Congress), 51 top (Will & Deni McIntyre), 15 (Gary Retherford), 35 (Bruce Roberts); Robertstock.com: 47 (M. Gibson), cover (J. Irwin), 45 (B. Krubner), 58 (R. Krubner), 71 top left (D. Petku), 71 right (Leonard Lee Rue III); Root Resources/Jana R. Jirak: 50; Stock Boston/John Elk III: 38; Stock Montage, Inc.: 21, 30 right; Transparencies Inc.: 55 (Billy E. Barnes), 4, 19 (Mike Boohar), 12 bottom (Bruce Clarke), 3 left, 3 right, 8, 9, 11, 18, 25 (Kelly Culpepper), 62 (Chuck Eaton), 51 bottom (Jane Faircloth), 36 right (J.E. Glenn), 68 (Chris Ippolito), 65 (Joe McLear), 16 (Les Saucier); Unicorn Stock Photos/Chuck Schmeiser: 66, 67; Visuals Unlimited/Gary W. Carter: 63.